Bird coloring book Vol 1, Vol2 and "The Chelsea Collection"

Illustrated by Emily Kate

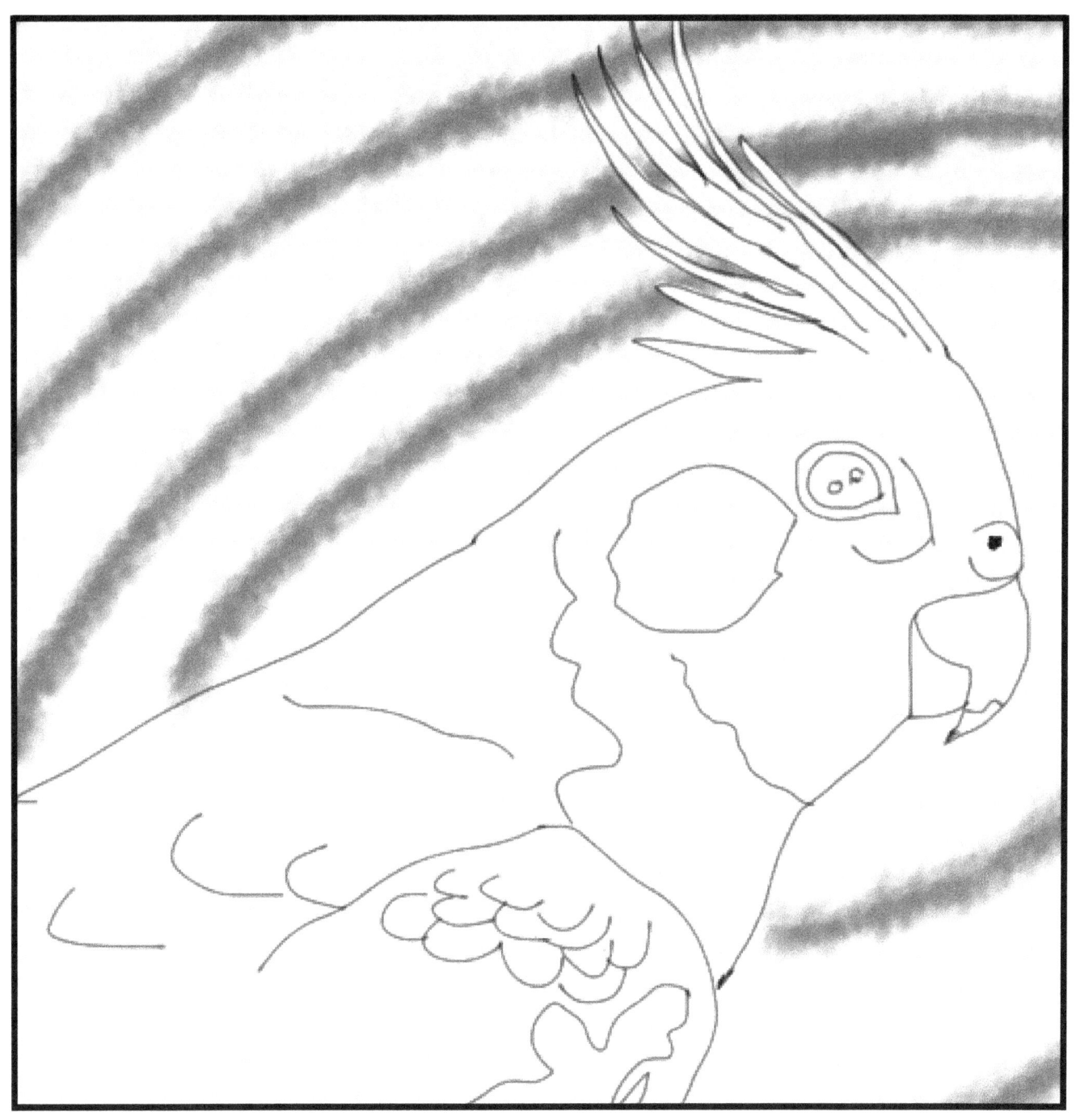

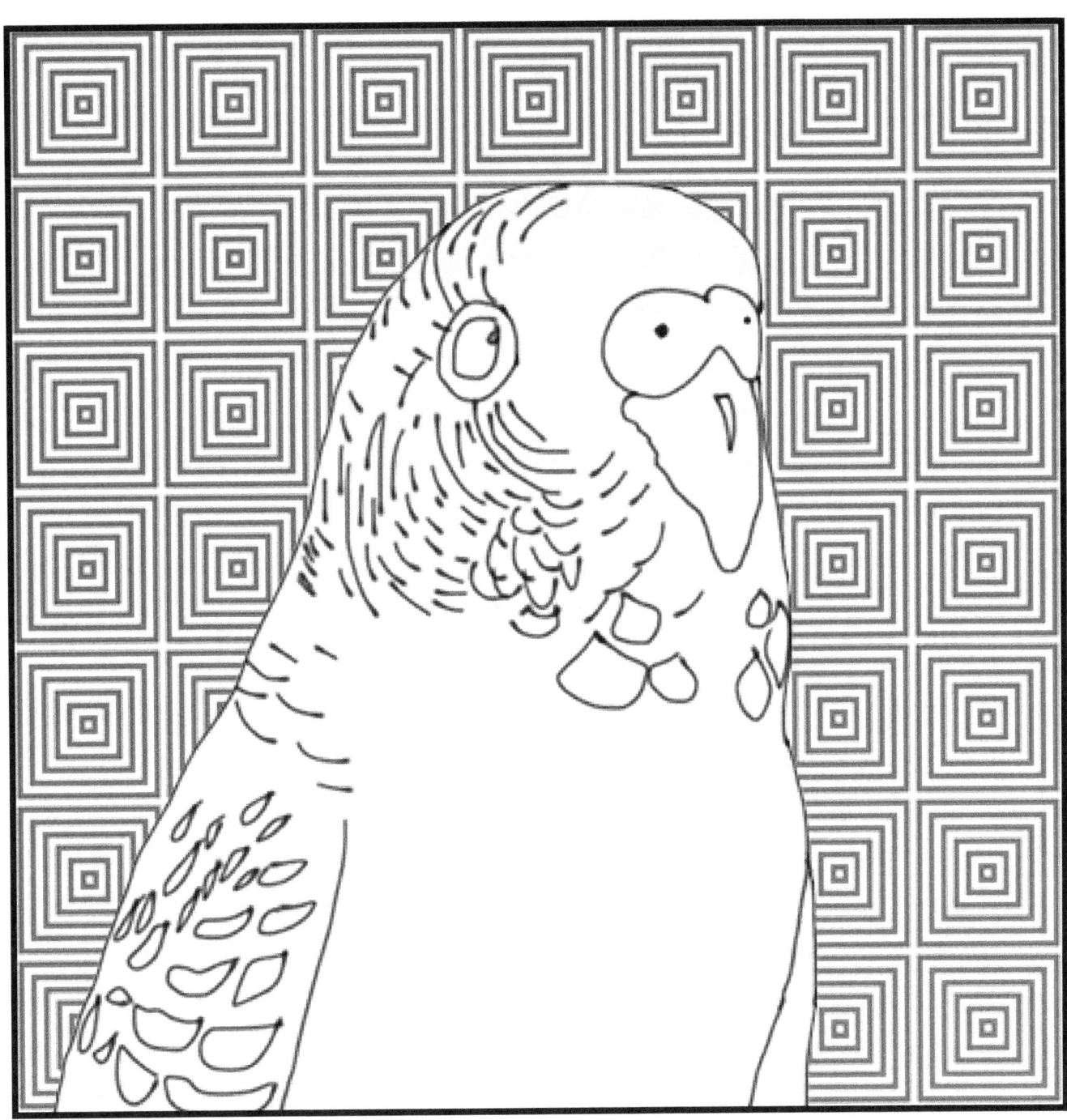

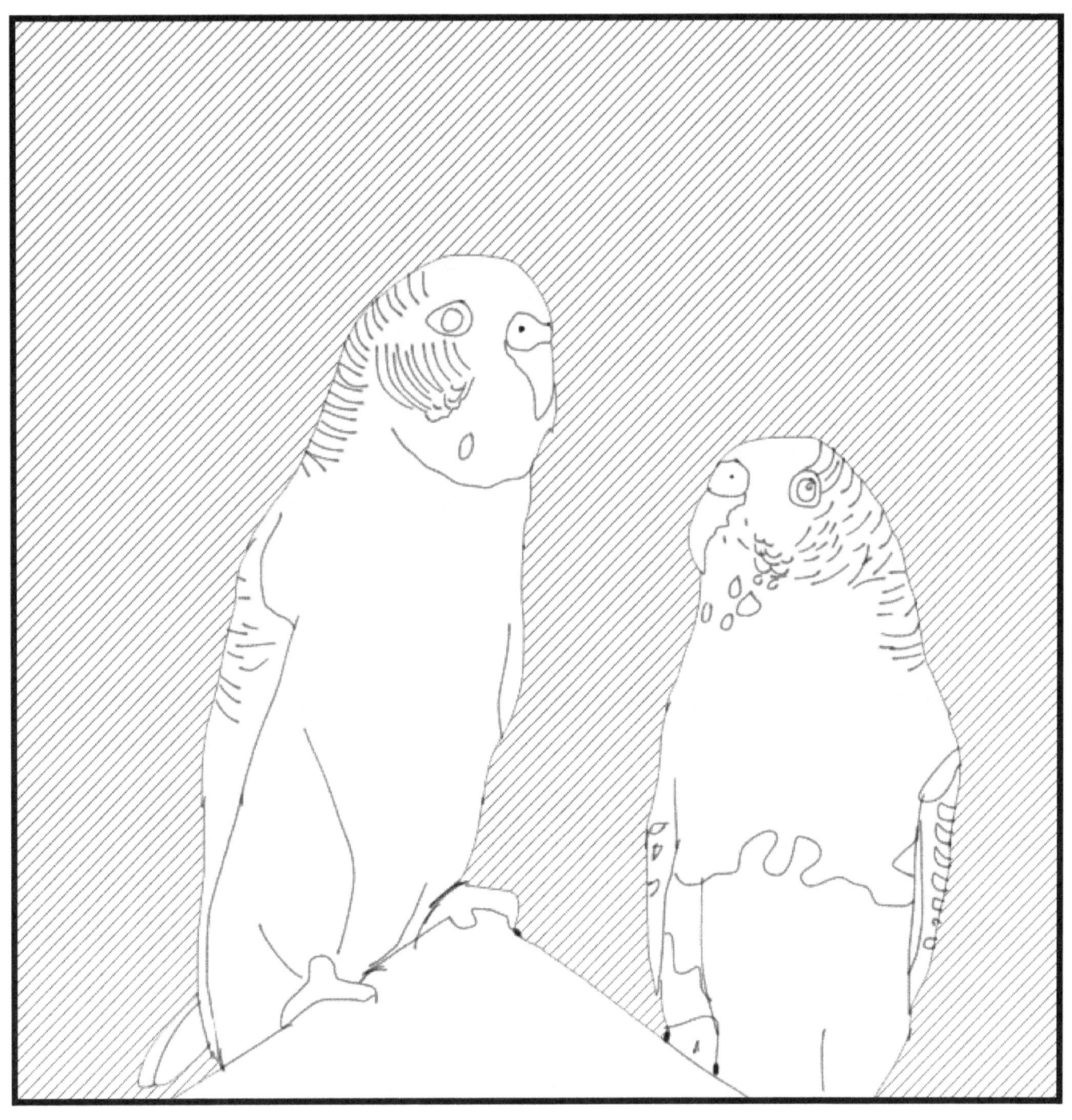

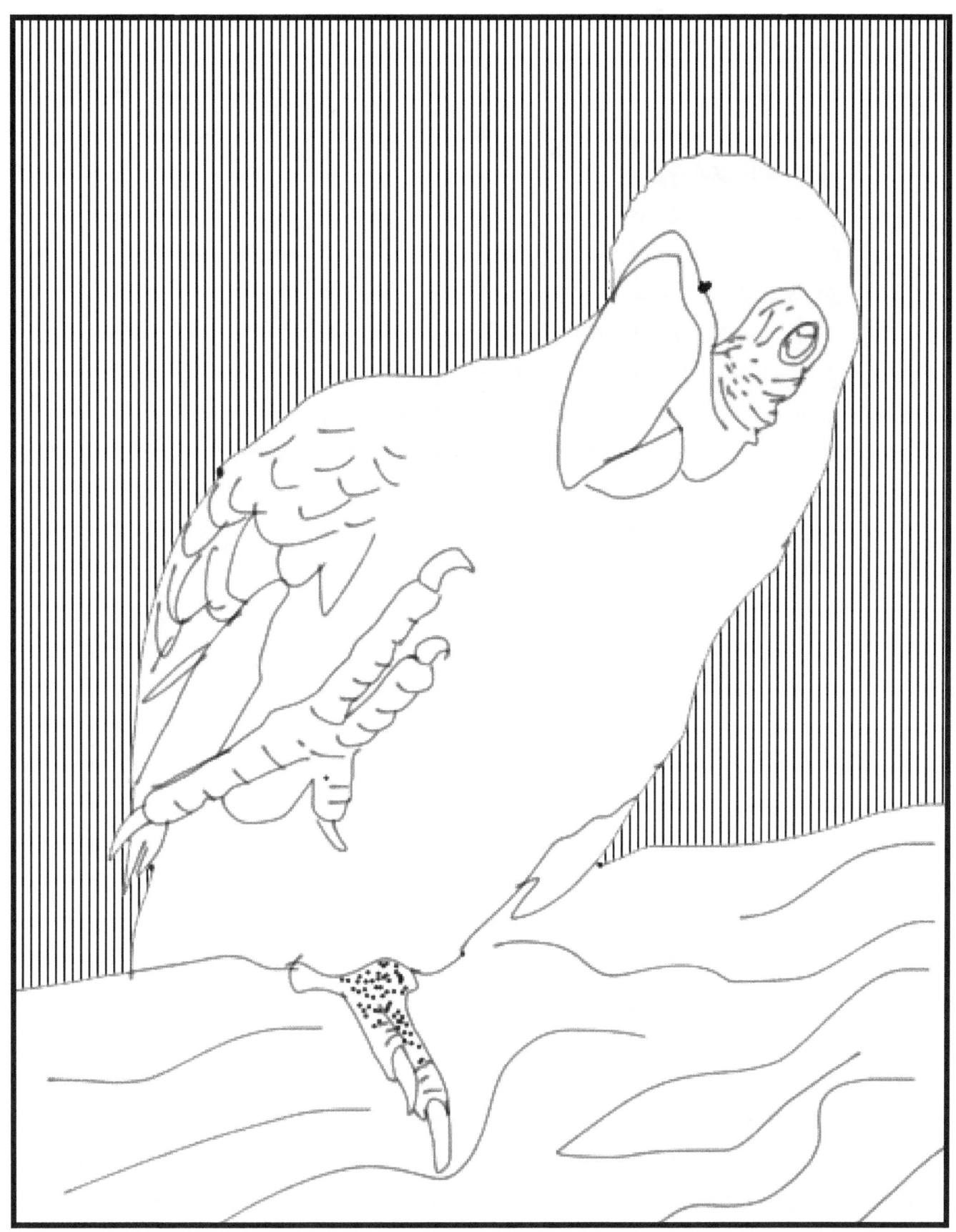

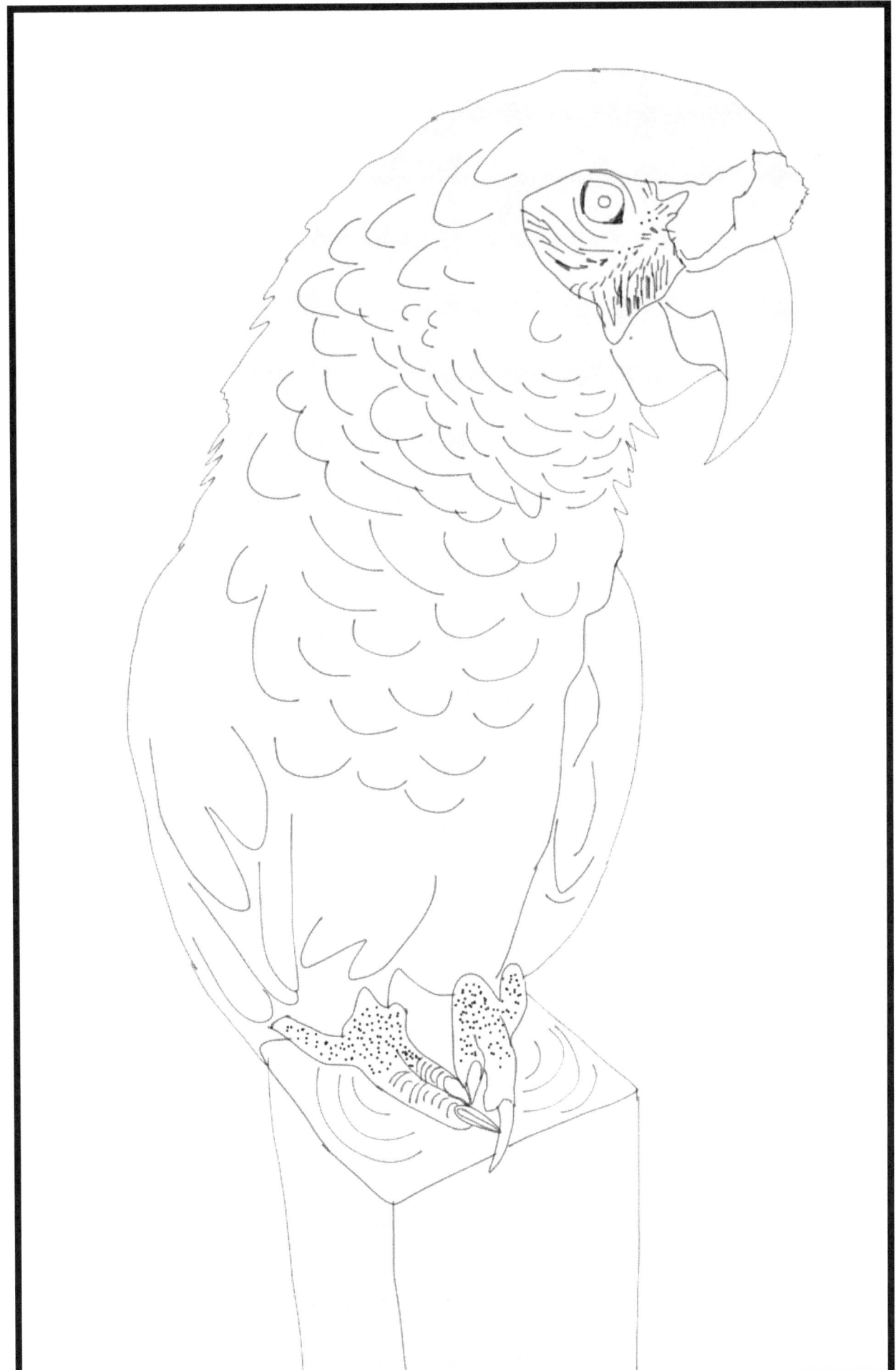

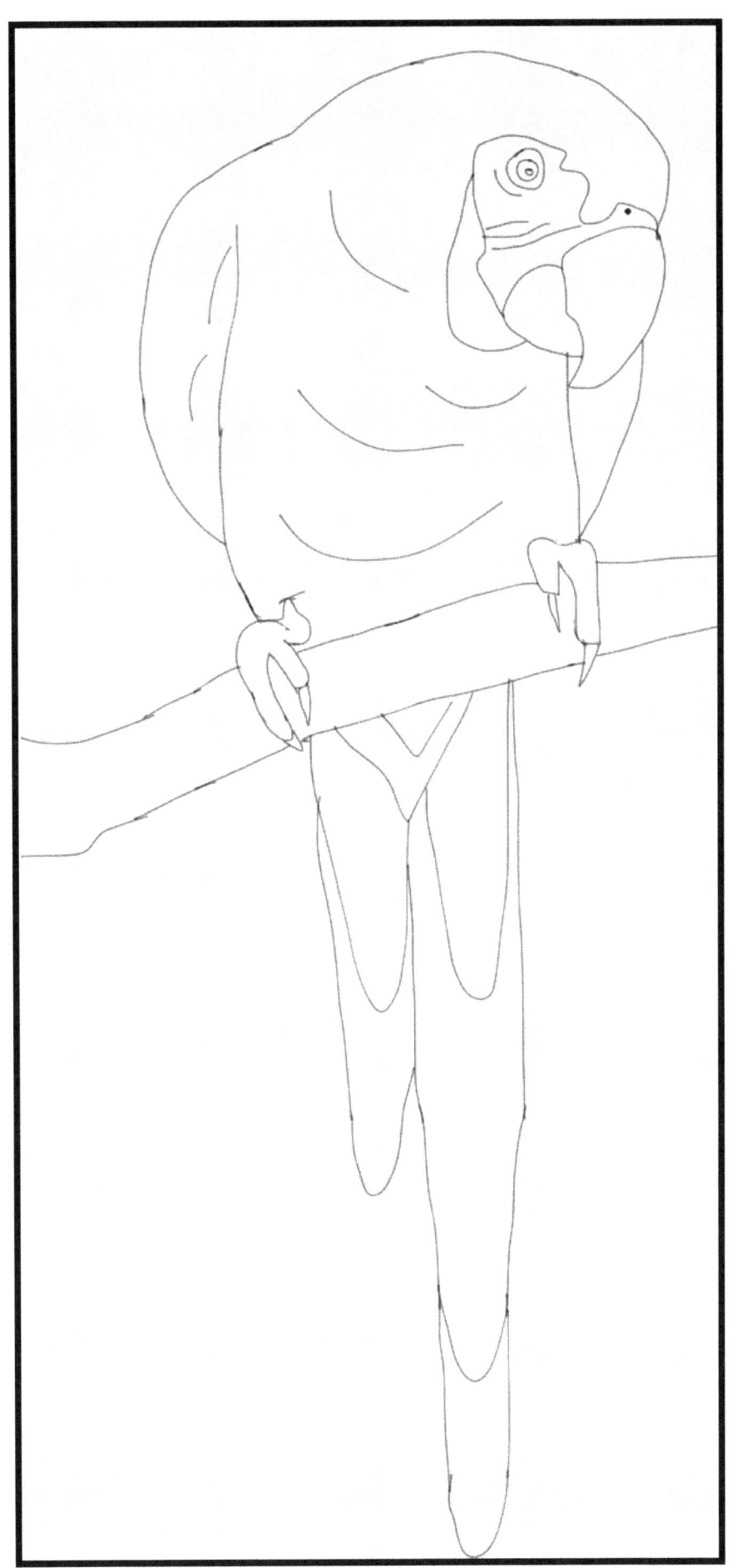

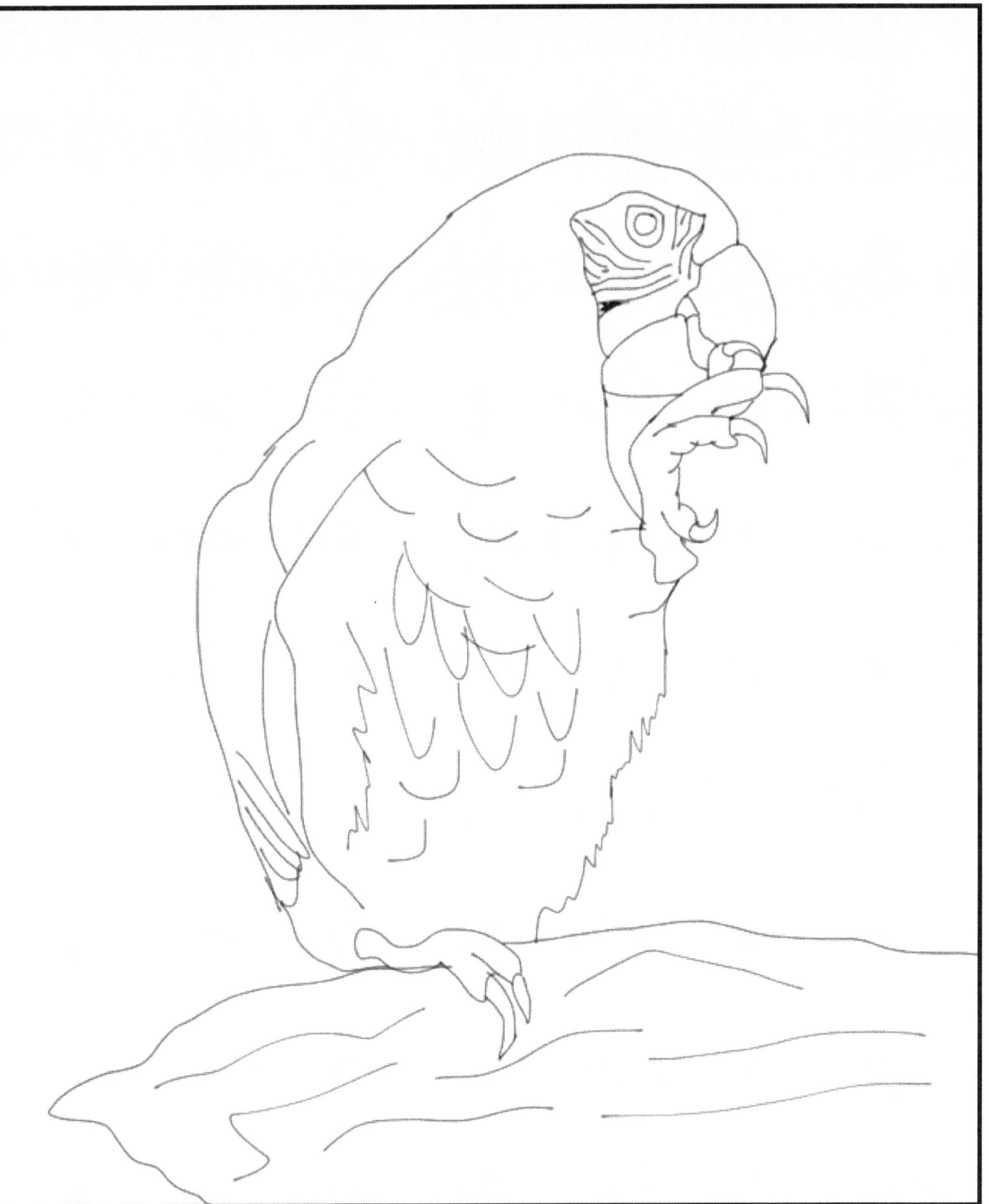

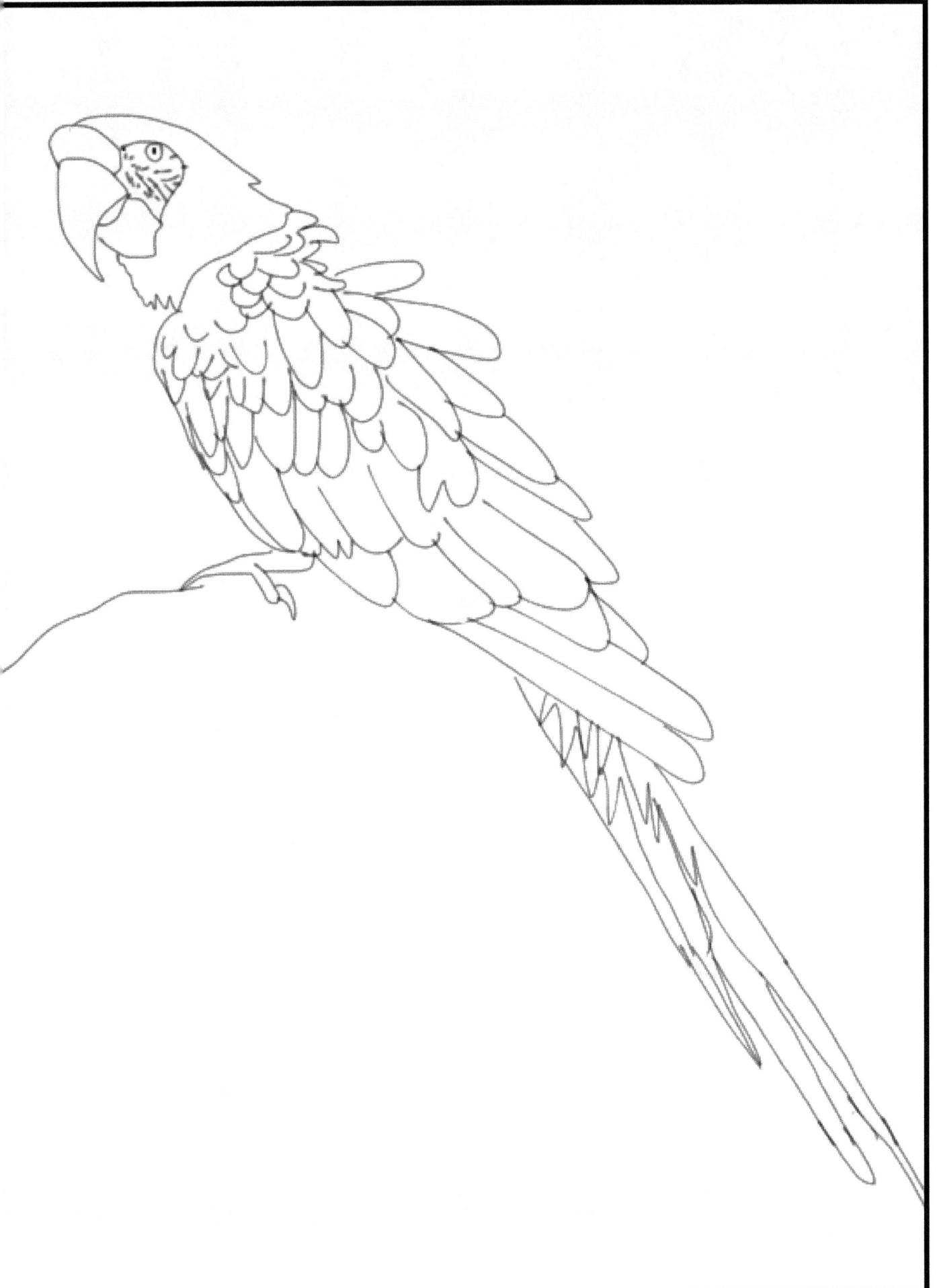

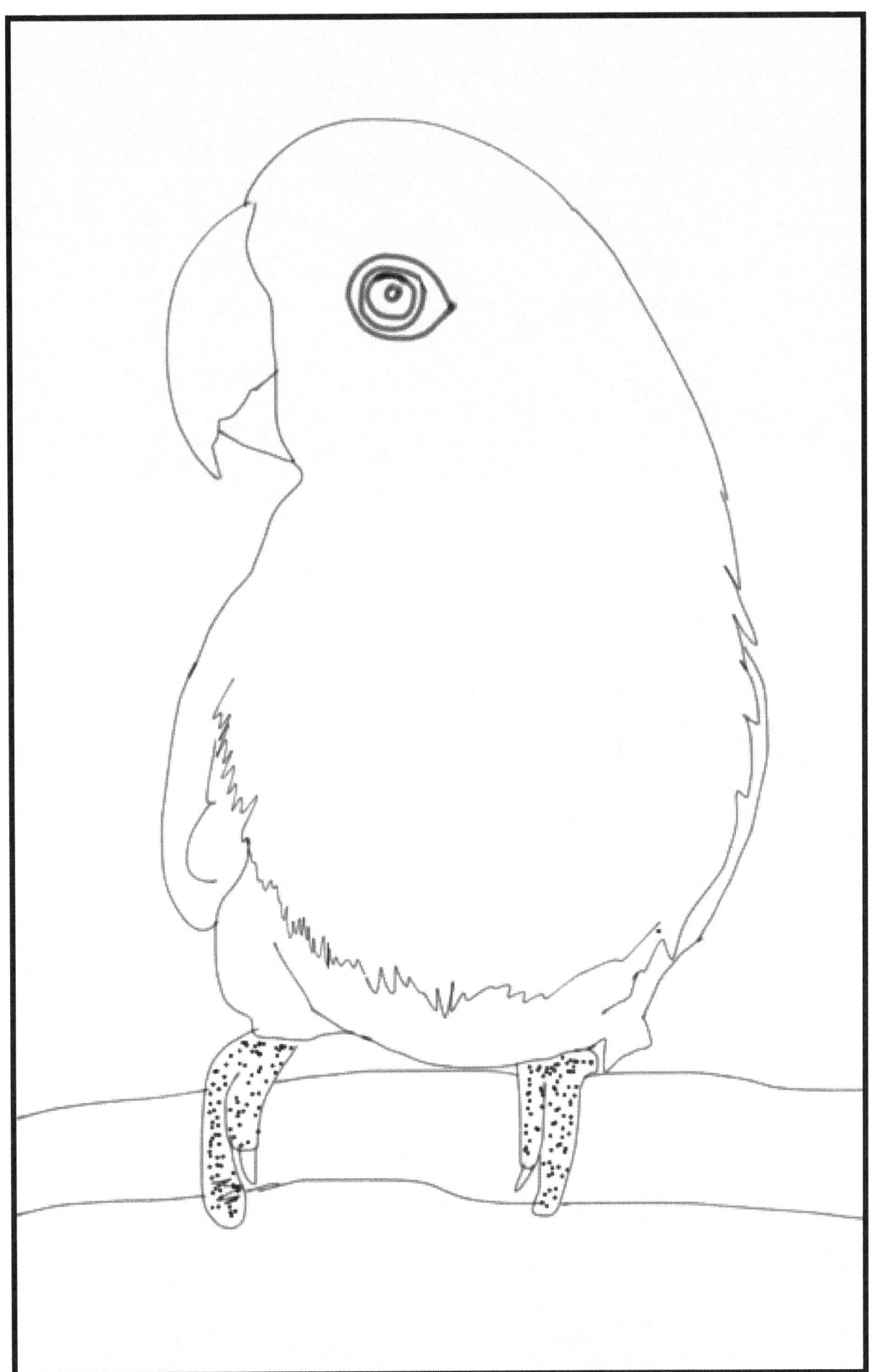

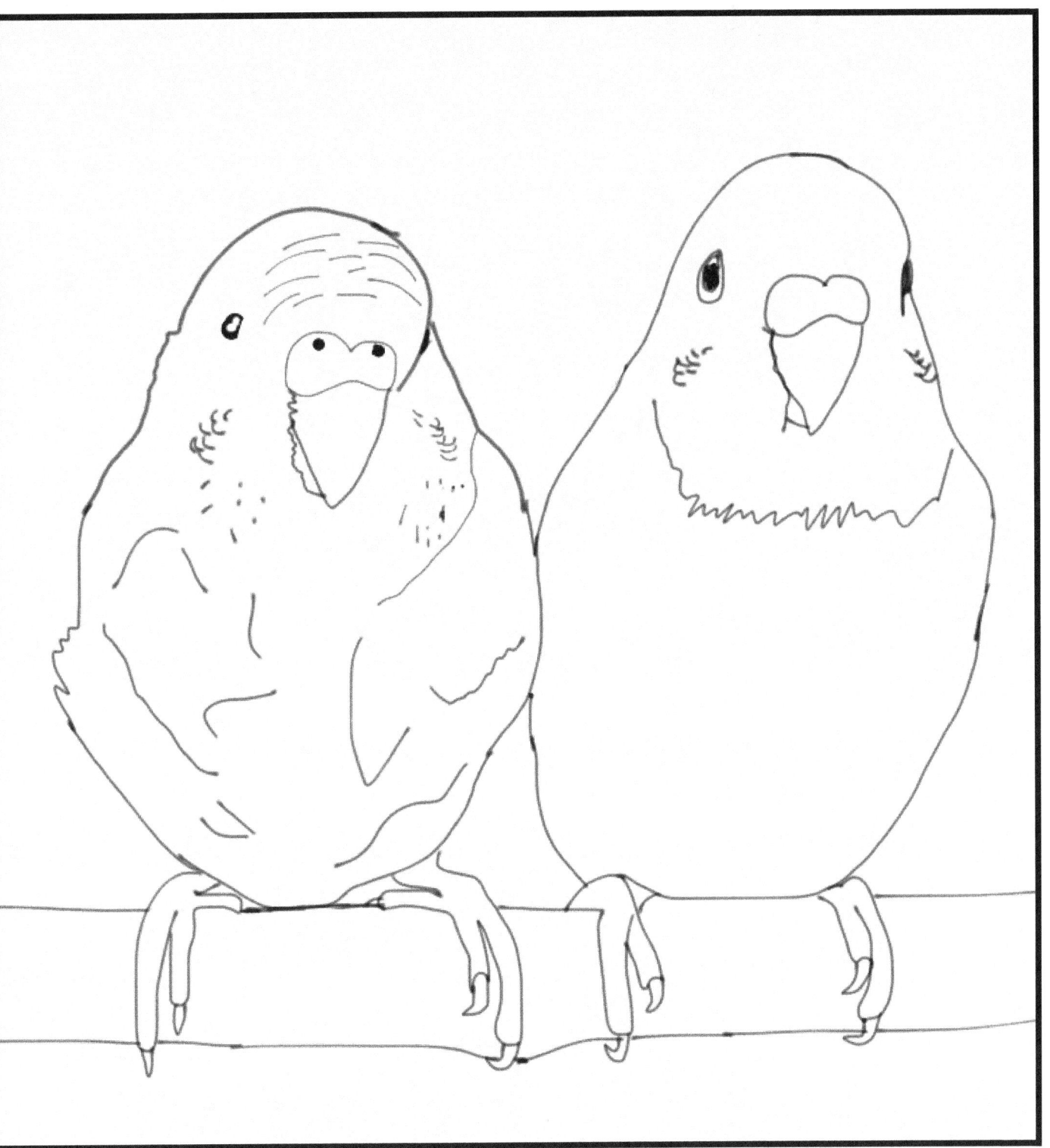

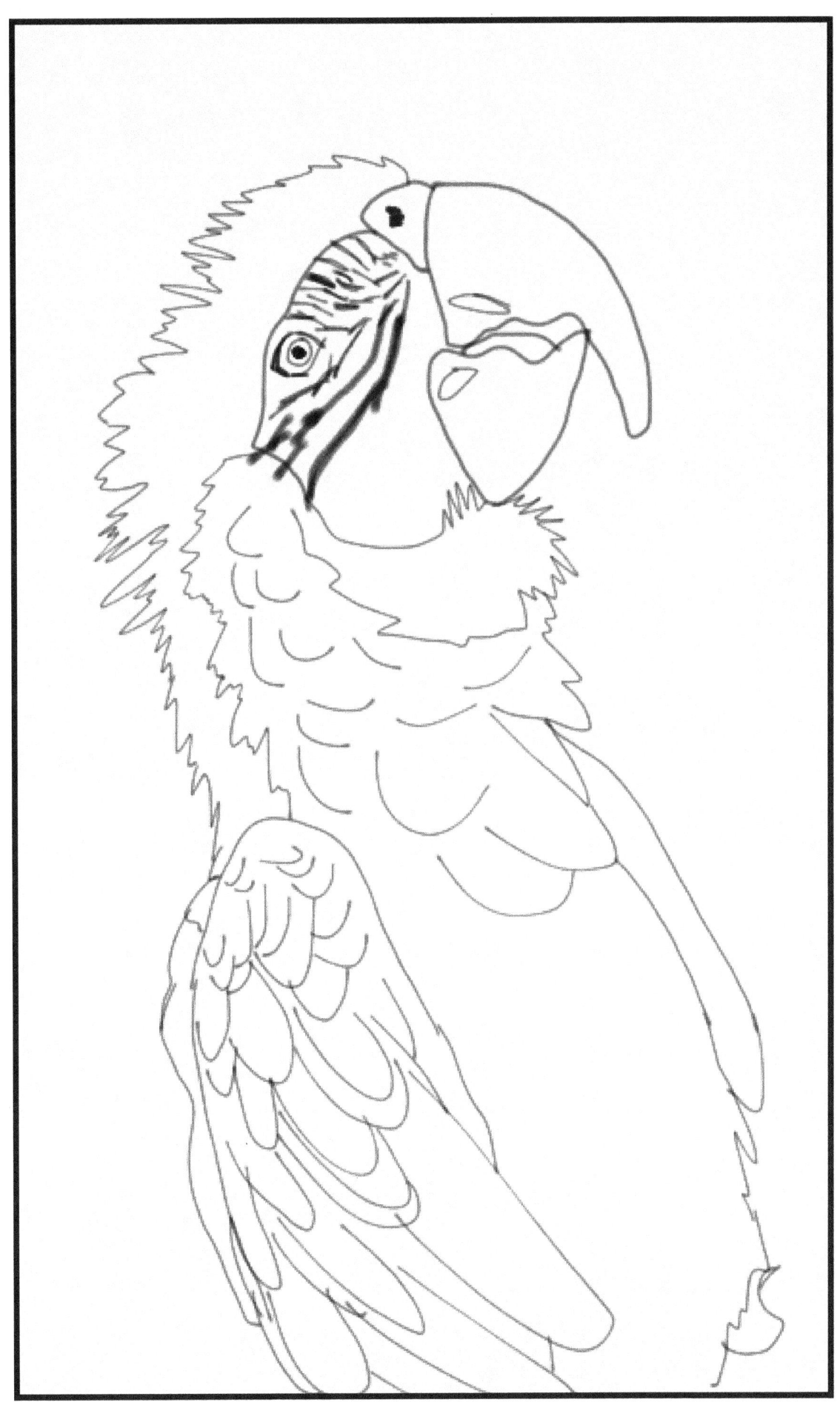

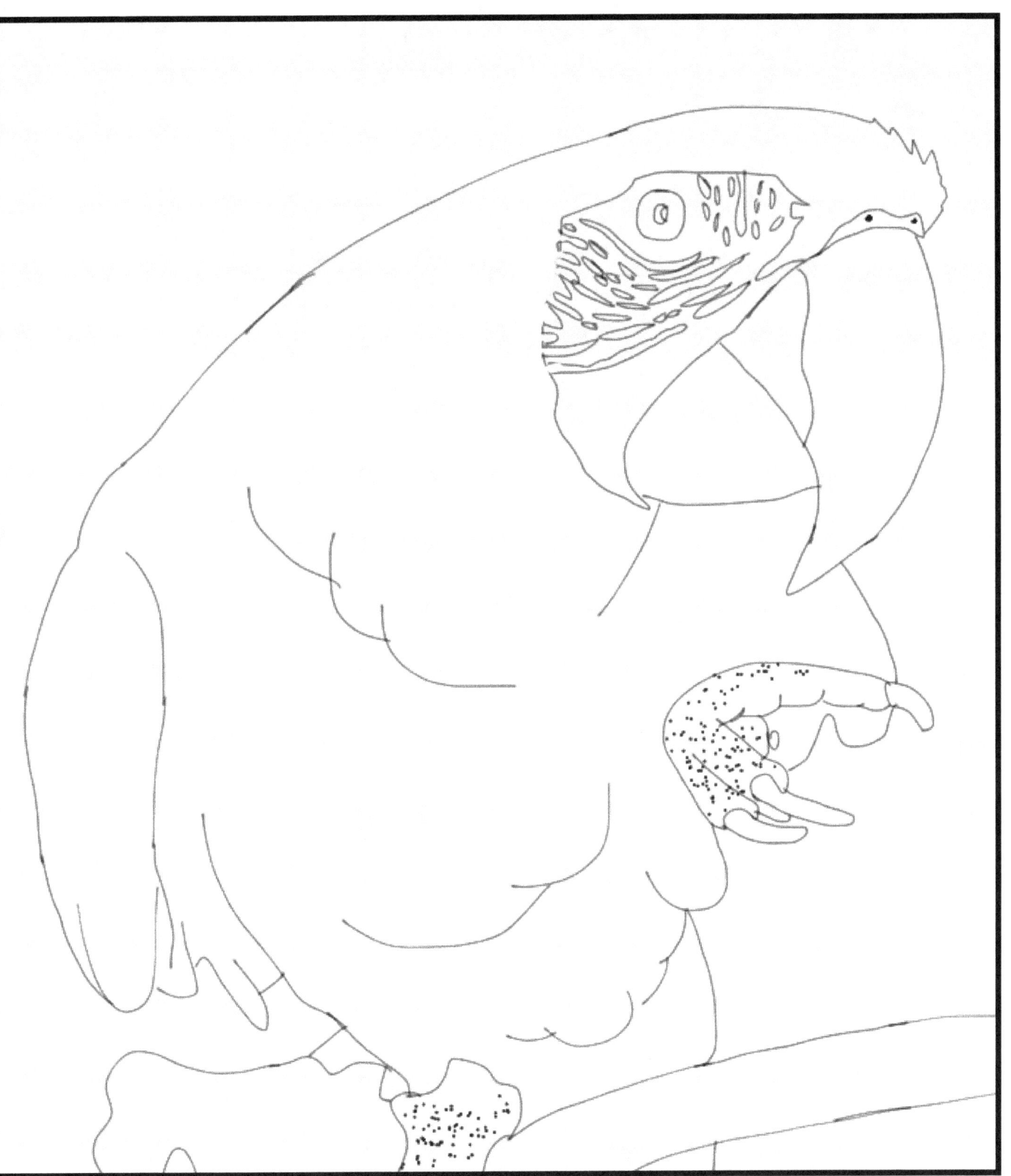

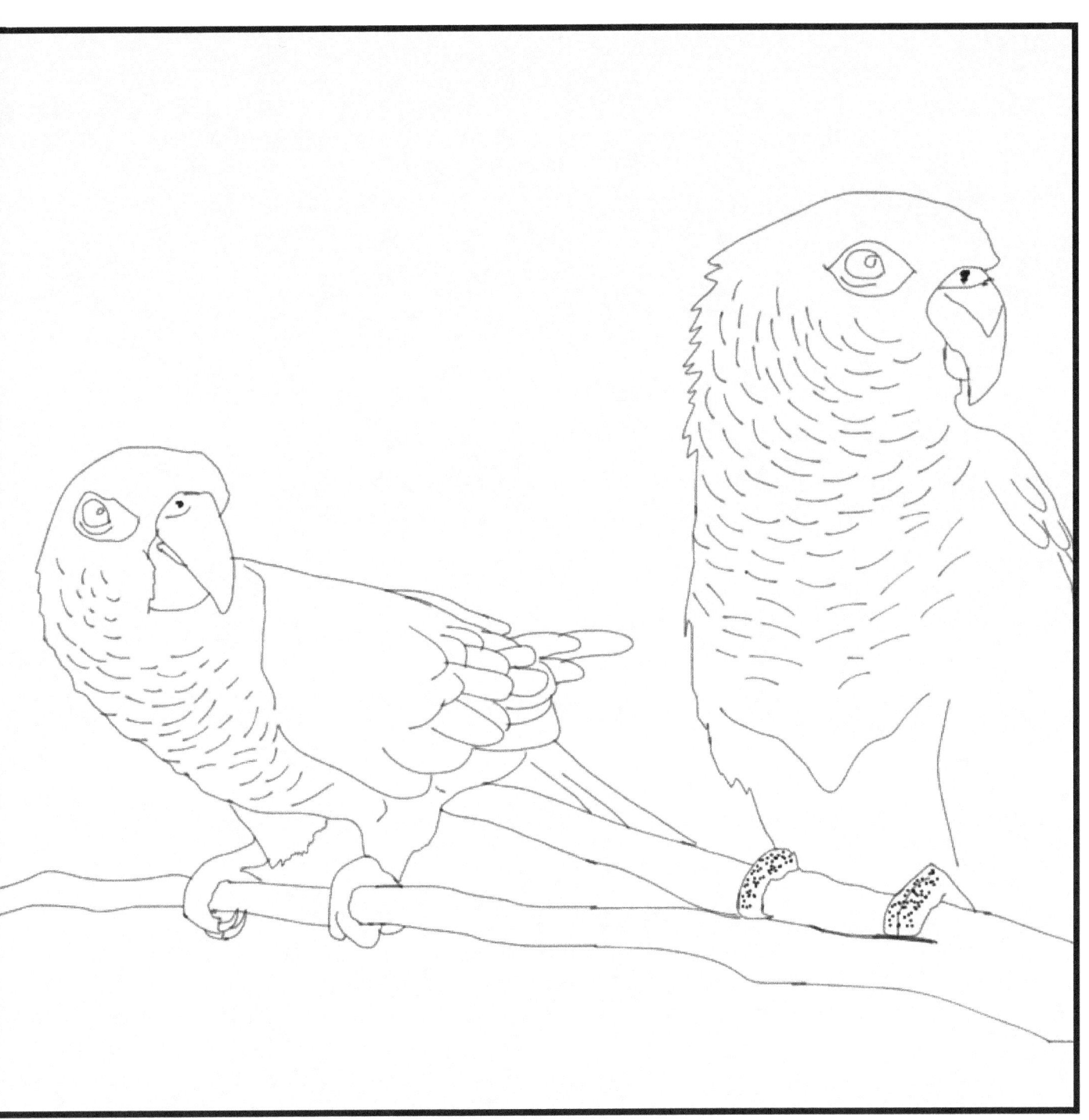

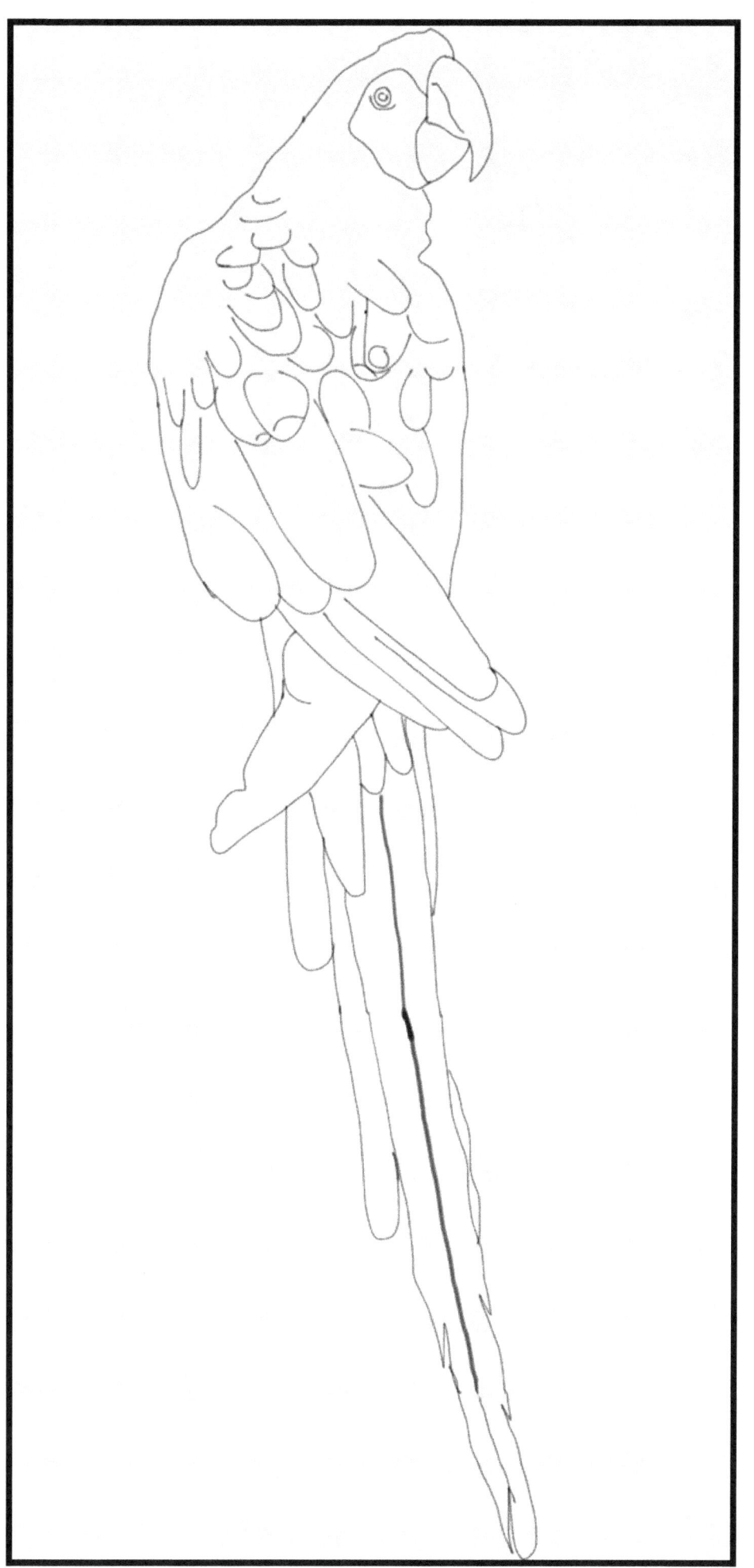

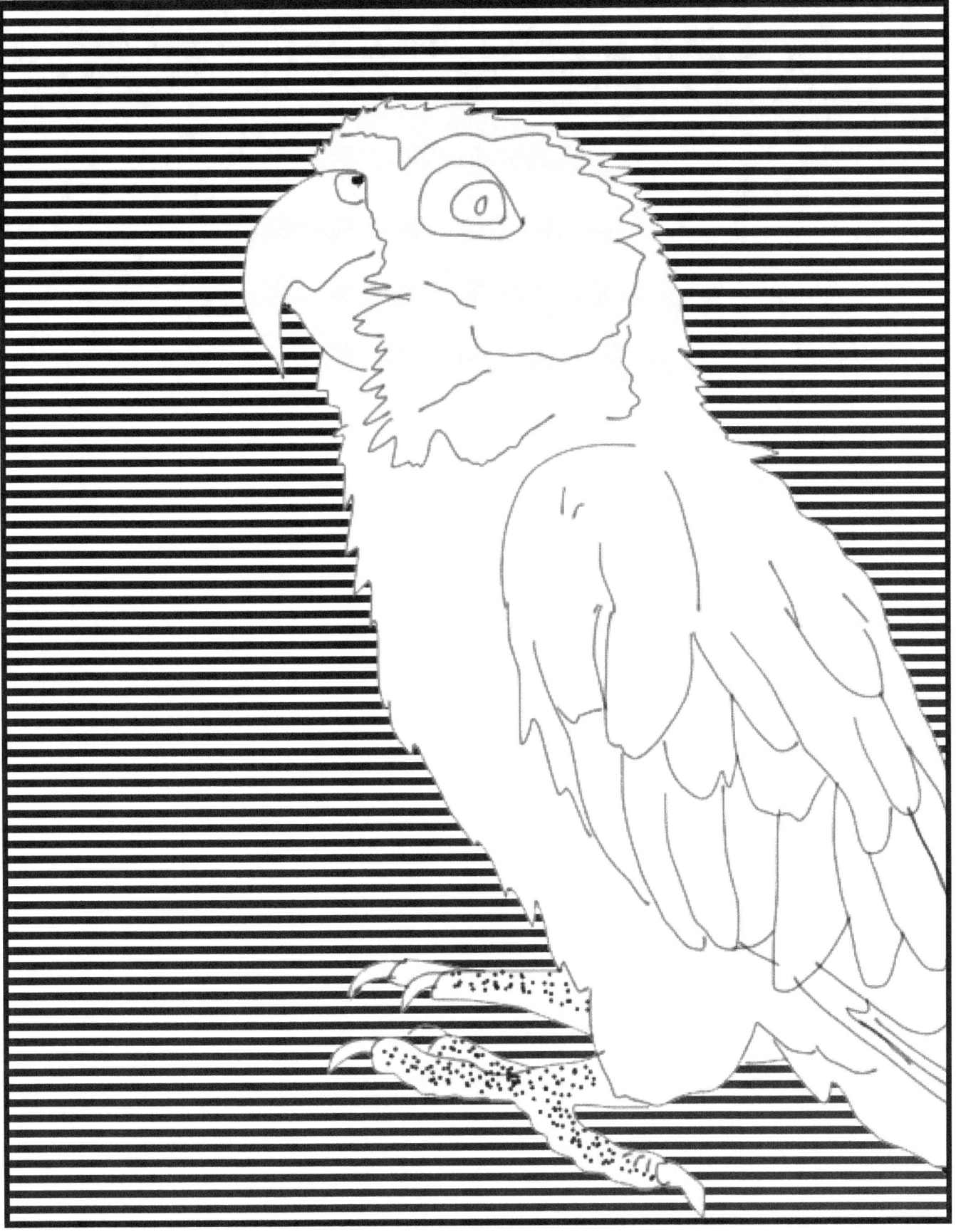

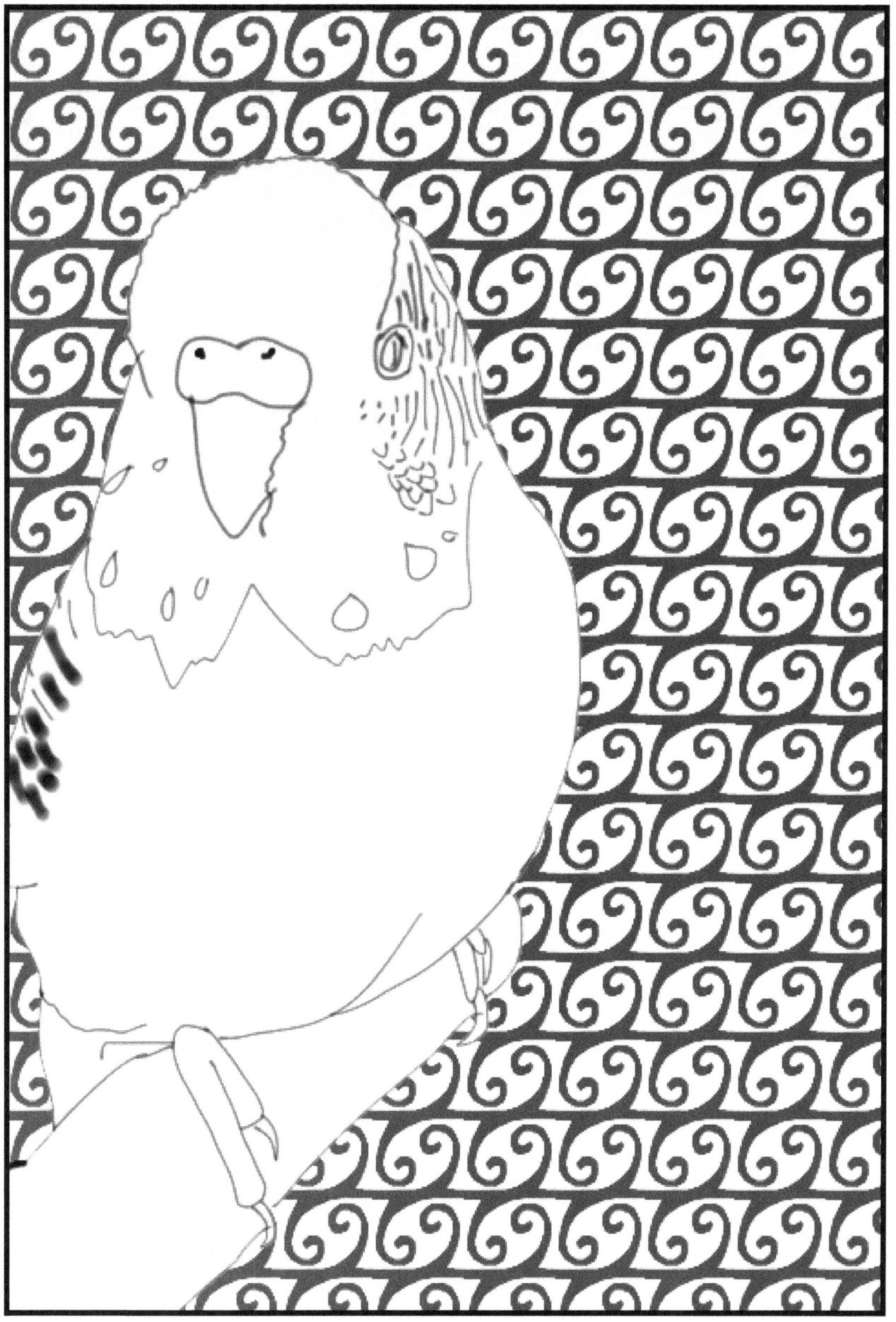

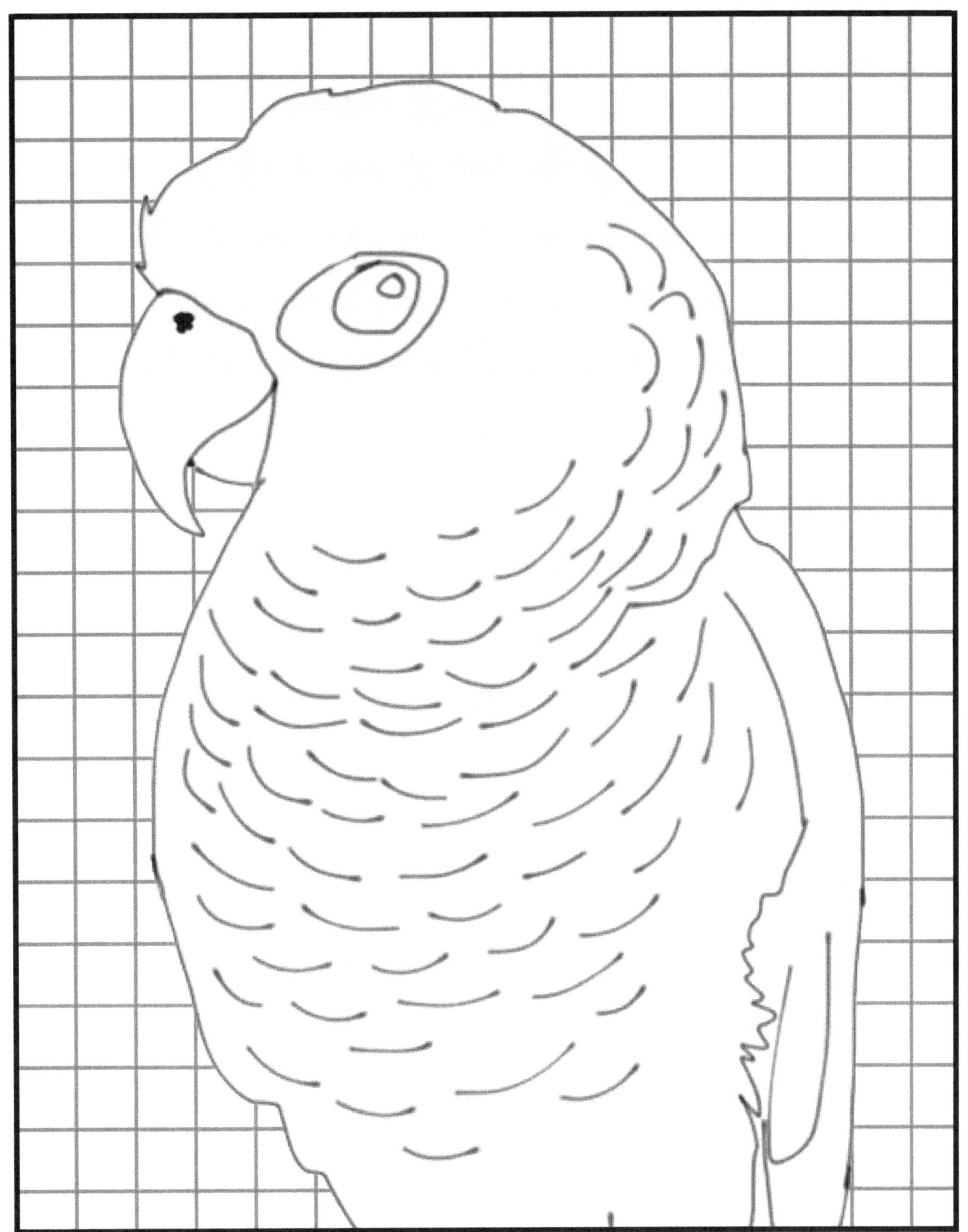

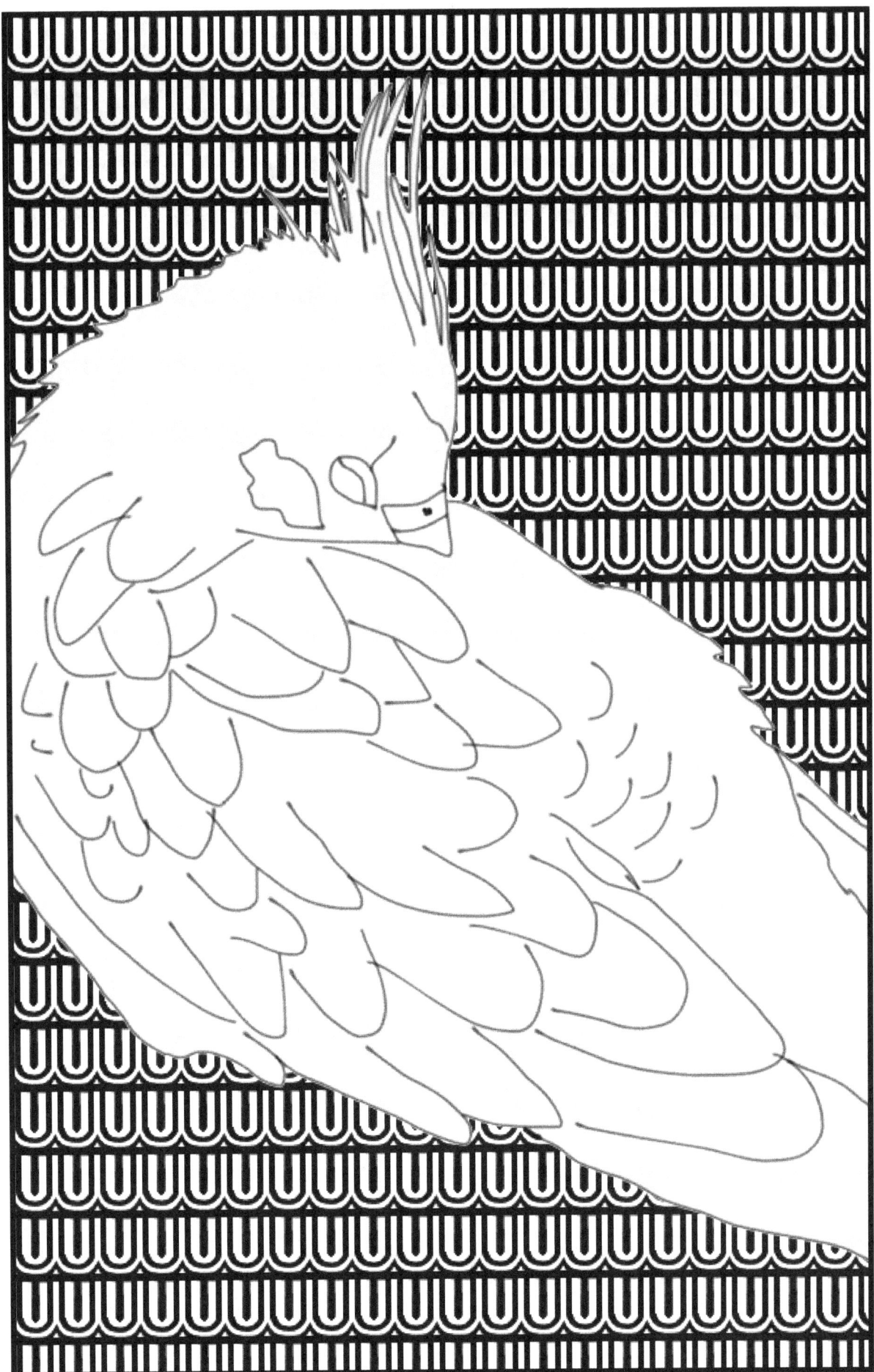

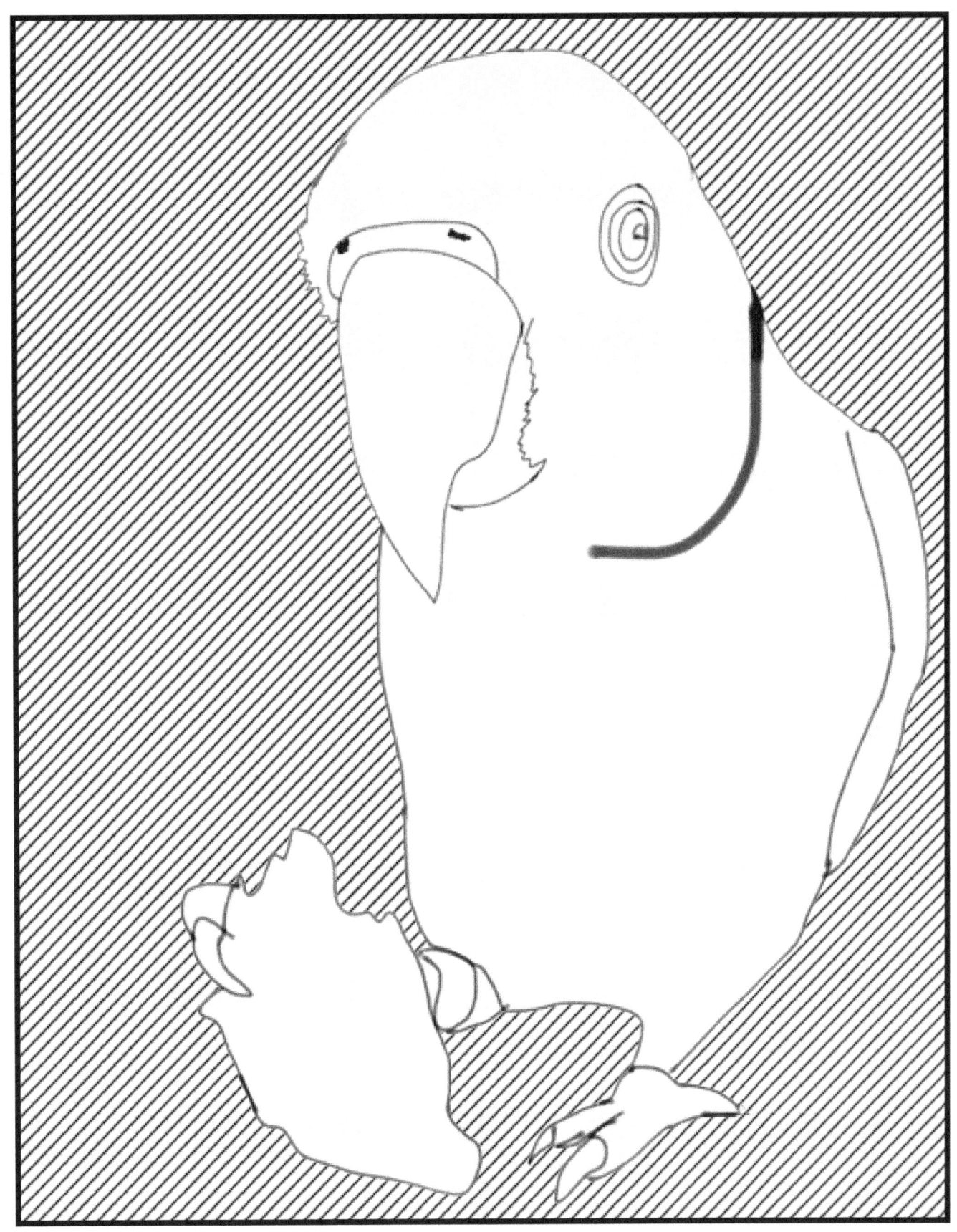

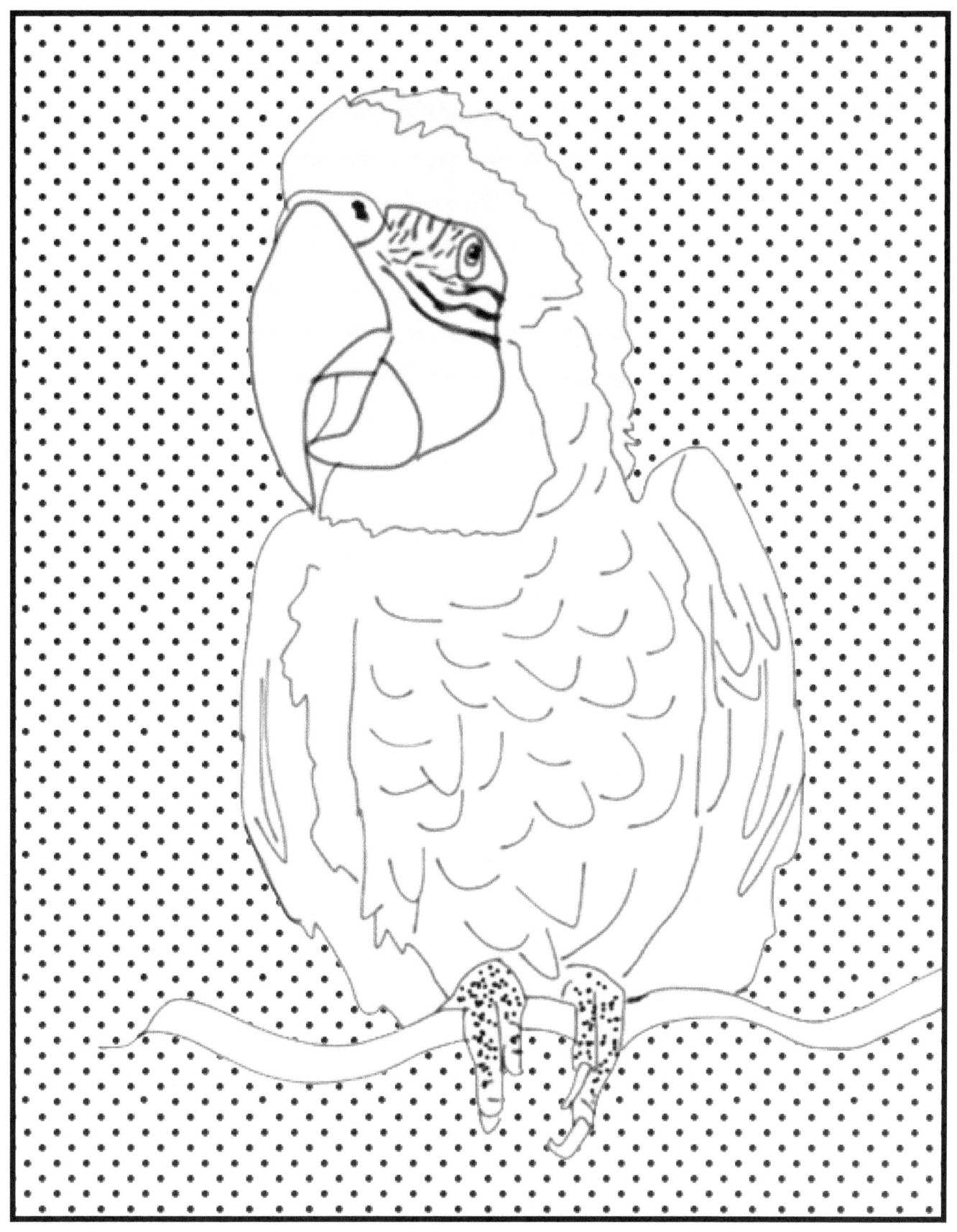

www.ingramcontent.com/pod-product-compliance
Lightning Source LLC
Chambersburg PA
CBHW081622220526

45468CB00010B/2994